Copyright © 2019 Alex Gibbons.

All rights reserved. No part of this publication may be reproduced, distributed or transmitted in any form or by any means, including photocopying, recording, or other electronic or mechanical methods, without the prior written permission of the publisher, except in the case of brief quotations embodied in critical reviews and certain other non-commercial uses permitted by copyright law.

Trademarked names appear throughout this book. Rather than use a trademark symbol with every occurrence of a trademarked name, names are used in an editorial fashion, with no intention of infringement of the respective owner's trademark. The information in this book is distributed on an "as is" basis, without warranty. Although every precaution has been taken in the preparation of this work, neither the author nor the publisher shall have any liability to any person or entity with respect to any loss or damage caused or alleged to be caused directly or indirectly by the information contained in this book.

A Portal To The Multiverse Within	3
Entering The Paradox	4
A Gate To Another World	5
Experiencing Death	8
A Brief History Of DMT Use	11
Chemistry, Pharmacology & Effects	15
Proper DMT Consumption	19
Proper Preparation	20
Instruments & Techniques	22
Important Tip	24
Extraction	25
Entering The Hallway Of All Possible Realities	26
DMT vs Other Psychedelics	29
DMT Culture	32
Therapeutic Effects On Anxiety & Depression	34
Bad Trips	36
The Cure For Collective Awareness?	39
Bonus: An Introductory Guide To Magic Mushrooms	43

A Portal To The Multiverse Within

The journey on DMT takes you to distant places that seem to be the point of intersection of multiple worlds. You may consider the experience to be a very personal one, a descent into your inner world and the discovery of the scenarios and creatures that populate it. But what people who took DMT describe, although unique for each individual in certain aspects, contains to many similarities to disregard the collective nature of this hallucinogenic experience.

Set yourself free of preconceptions, and if this is a hard thing to do nowadays, know that, in what concerns DMT, spirituality as well as science are on the same page. Take a step forward towards accepting and containing all of yourself, all that is. Let this book be your guide into the mysteries of this miraculous compound, and follow it to discover the profound and complex potential of your own consciousness.

Entering The Paradox

The effect of DMT is hard to describe in metaphors, hyperboles, oxymorons and similes because it is the expression of the essential paradox of life. As it's been portrayed, DMT reveals the matrix of reality and plunges you into the multiverse, into the vast infinite dimensional realm of parallel realities. Neither perception nor clarity of mind are distorted but heightened.

What each understands from this unearthly endeavor is, though, mostly personal. Some have healed past traumas, others have overcome addictions and great fears, most have faced their denials and understood why their lives unrolled the way they did and what their purpose in this existence is now. What is common for all reports from users is the state of enlightenment and the unbelievable expansion of consciousness.

A Gate To Another World

DMT is an omnipresent molecule, embedded in the chemical structure of virtually all living organisms. If you can imagine that this outstanding compound that has the potential of offering you the experience of infinite lifetimes in just a few minutes, is extractable from mere grass then you can start to grasp its magic. As the saying goes, the greatest treasures of the world are hidden under your eyes, so take a step out and a better look at your lawn. Look at the flowers, the trees, the ants in the ground and the birds in the sky. Look at your dog, at the mosquito you just squashed, look at yourself. DMT is everywhere you look.

Of course dimethyltryptamine is not the only recurrent substance in both plants and animals, but for now, no other one has been found to provoke such a mind-blowing and life-changing effect when consumed. No other one to reveal the substance of life, the intricate connection bonding space and time and all living things. Could it be that DMT's pervasive nature is signaling us that we are indeed all one, a single united consciousness? Can DMT tackle the contemporary problem of singularity?

The syntagm that became the stamp to define this incredible compound, 'the spirit molecule' is referring to the spiritual dimension that DMT awakens, the connection with a higher force, with the prime source of energy. By igniting a complete sense of awareness, it reveals the universal blueprint of life. Yet, this is not schematic knowledge that can be translated in words or scientific terms, we don't have the proper concepts in order to explain this type of information.

It goes beyond the characters and events you meet during the trip, and can only be contained by the state of spirit that's induced in you, because if you were to analyze the mind-boggling endeavors that people recount having after consuming DMT, you would be inquiring the immense basin of archetypal stories that mankind ever imagined. But the essential aspect is that these fairytale stories, even though resembling hallucinations or dreams, were vividly experienced, with an awakened mind, clear, utterly attentive and perceptive, with all the senses heightened and feeling completely new sensations.

This type of sensitivity is unprecedented not only in all first-time users but also in all human experience in the course of history. It could be assimilated as a most powerful religious experience, or in modern terms, as a true spiritual awakening, but both these concepts are not extensive enough to contain what one lives when taking DMT. And this is mainly because the DMT trip feels much more real than both, it's as if you were sensing multiple dimensions of reality that have not been addressed by any of the literature that's been generated by humans till the present moment.

Moreover, it's as if you were sensing this multiverse with senses that you couldn't have dreamed of possessing, while totally unable to define the experience using the rational predicaments we are used to. The DMT journey is therefore a complex phenomenon that surpasses and defies the scientific laws and religious scriptures.

Nonetheless, this new wave of consciousness is gaining momentum with more and more adepts, and gradually yet rapidly building around it a new narrative. This is the narrative of the new men. In this line of thought, can we talk about the DMT culture in terms of a new religion? Even if we are merely taking the first steps in this next generation of thinking and perceiving reality, we might as well call it that.

The most important change that this DMT culture is bringing to our consciousness is the bridging of religion and science, the two disciplines that have guided human evolution to where we are now, while being in constant conflict with each other. We've already sketched the spiritual dimension that you are submerged in when doing DMT, but what is more spectacular is that it describes the key concepts that quantum physics is working with.

During the DMT trip you have the sensation that time and space warp in a continuum dimension, or in other words, that there is no past or future but an eternal present and that space is infinite. Moreover, this type of environment grants you the ability to be everywhere in this very moment, the same way in which quantum physics explains that the laws of the microcosmos allow the molecules to be in more places in the same time. In this sense, you could say that DMT is actually bending the structure and ordinary dynamics of your mind in order to accept the existence of multiple layers of reality and an infinite potential of manifestation. Simply said, this would mean to accept the inherent paradox of life.

Experiencing Death

DMT has been associated with the concept and experience of death in many ways, starting with the idea that became a meme, stating that DMT is produced by the body at the moment of death, which is a plausible and provocative speculation, but not yet a proven fact.

This concept has been pushed extensively since the launch of 'The spirit molecule' book and documentary, where Dr. Rick Strassman, its author, is suggesting that this compound may be released by our bodies when entering special states of consciousness like meditation, sleep, trance or death. Furthermore, this movie, as well as the research in this subject, have inquired the individual experiences of different people who confessed their out-of-body journeys on DMT were indeed, feeling as if they had died.

The DMT trip propels your consciousness out of the ordinary presence, out of your body, cutting the connection with the material dimension. The trance that you enter, although extremely short, is enrapturing you in a completely different state of being, where your perception is not anymore guided by your five senses, but from a central point within your being, by the inner sense of awareness.

The worlds that you travel through are perceived in a totally different manner because you are sensing everything as raw as it is, unobstructed by the inherent limitations of our five senses, and neither by the predetermined understanding of our minds. As such, DMT takes you in an exploration of new territories, in which you find yourself a new being, using new instruments of guidance. Of course, in a realm where space and time are superfluous, where the entire spectrum of vision is distorted and populated with dream-like visions, the feeling that you are not anymore on this planet, becomes more than reasonable.

The strong sense of detachment from the physical plane, amplified by the inability to receive stimuli from the physical reality while you are submerged in the inner journey, is contributing substantially to the impression that you've just died.

But there are other substances that induce a similar detachment, ketamine is one of the synthetic compounds that present such an effect, and there's also a number of plant medicines that fall into the same category, among which are peyote, iboga or psychedelic mushrooms. They're not however associated with death as much as DMT is.

This is due to DMT's modus operandi, the dynamic through which it cuts your connections to materiality not only by pausing your senses of orientation but also by collapsing your entire mental structure, your ego. This is the essential shock that one goes through and that creates the powerful illusion of dying. By dissolving your identity, DMT is in fact erasing what you are used to calling you, and the great surprise is that without an identity, your consciousness continues to exist. This occurrence, termed as 'ego death' has been intensively inquired as it has important implications from philosophical as well as scientific points of view, starting with the question of what exactly is consciousness, and if there is life after death.

Most of the people that took DMT report coming back from this presumed death, with a feeling of an intense spiritual awakening that left them with the comforting sensation that life may continue after we die. But the conviction that the conscious ego will dwell further than our flesh is apparently nothing more than a whimsical hope. Nonetheless, DMT proves that our consciousness is not bounded by our ego and that our sense of awareness does not depend upon our individuality.

DMT tackles this fundamental question of humanity, what happens after we die, a problem that men have tried to get a vision of through all possible means, that has been interpreted by religion, philosophy and science in multiple scenarios. What's all the more spectacular is that the DMT trip, like the near-death experiences, produces very similar visions. People recount having the same sense of detachment from their bodies, seeing a tunnel that sweeps them into a bright white light, and taking them to dreamlike realms where they met entities of light, which the more religious of them describe as saints.

So, it seems reasonable that dimethyltryptamine is associated with death and furthermore it can be a unique way in which you can confront your fear of death. But is it actually threatening your life? Can DMT induce death? The answer is no. The quantity of substance that is enough to produce one very strong trip is far from endangering your health. What the famous psychonaut Terence Mckenna had to say about this issue was that death can occur in a DMT experience only if 'death by astonishment' is possible.

A Brief History Of DMT Use

The use of trance medicinal plants containing DMT goes far back down our historic timeline than the actual synthesization of the compound by modern chemists. Its original use was traced to South America, but considering that it was primarily employed by tribal cultures that had no other means to register their knowledge and history but through oral communication, we actually have no certainty that DMT based plants were not consumed in other parts of the world as well.

The well-known Amazonian hallucinogenic brew Ayahuasca is made from the leaves of the Chacruna plant, Psychotria Viridis, or the Chagropanga plant, Diplopterys Cabrerana, that contain high concentrations of DMT, combined with the Banisteriopsis Caapi vine, which brings to the whole compound a most necessary addition.

The tropical vine is included in the drink to prolong the trance effect because it contains harmine, a substance that inhibits the breakdown of the dimethyltryptamine by our digestive system. This explains why the Ayahuasca trance takes as long as eight to nine hours, compared with the DMT trip which is about fifteen minutes, of which the highest state lasts for only five. This will be more clearly explained in the next chapter when we'll be discussing the chemical processes occurring in the body with the intake of this compound.
It's important to remember that Amazonian cultures knew the way DMT worked long before it became popular among modern civilization. The earliest records of the traditional use of DMT containing plants date from the 8th century when it

was apparently utilized to produce psychoactive snuffs, as the cohoba for example, made from the seeds of Anadenanthera Peregrina.

But even in South America Ayahuasca was restricted to tribal cultures as it caught the interest of the wider public and started to spread when the rubber industry exploded in the Amazon and opened a door through which civilization entered the jungle and traditional knowledge, in exchange, stepped in the urban environment.

The enthusiasm with the medicine brew was so big that it spawned an entire religion, a series of Ayahuasca cults appearing in Brazil, merging the traditional beliefs of the Amazons with the Brazilian cosmology and Catholicism. The first Ayahuasca religion, Santo Daime, was founded in 1930, and after the seventies it started to expand to other continents, today is recognized as an established spiritual cult that is permitted to use its main Ayahuasca ritual in many countries of the world.

The chemical DMT was first discovered and synthesized in 1931 by Richard Manske, a Canadian chemist, but at that moment nothing else was known about this compound. Then in 1946, Oswaldo Goncalves de Lima, a microbiologist, found that DMT is naturally occurring in plants. But it wasn't until ten years later, in 1956, that Stephen Szara made it known of the psychoactive effects of the substance.

The Hungarian chemist and psychiatrist became familiar with DMT during his travels to South America where he participated in traditional religious ceremonies with plant medicine and remained fascinated. He then extracted DMT from the Mimosa Hostilis plant and injected himself with the compound intramuscularly, and his discoveries spawned the Western curiosity regarding this mind-altering substance and the medicinal and hallucinogenic cultures of the Amazon.

In 1965 Franzen and Gross discovered that DMT was to be found in the urine and blood of humans. This finding, sent them on a misleading route, as they suspected the occurrence of DMT within our bodies was related to mental imbalances such as schizophrenia. The explanation was that this condition may be the effect of a metabolic error of the human body, which produced this type of hallucinogen and thus sickened the brain.

Of course, the studies produced no hard evidence to link dimethyltryptamine with the respective mental condition, but fortunately it triggered the scientific interest towards the amazing effects on consciousness and the extraordinary ways in which it interacts with the normal dynamics of the brain.

The ecstatic hippie period of the 60's and 70's provided a fertile context for the research into the effects of DMT, and a great number of papers were produced by prominent figures of the time like Alan Watts and Timothy Leary, a body of work that more than anything else, marked the first steps into the modern study of consciousness. The set back came in 1970 when the Controlled Substances Act was to pause any further research into DMT, or other psychedelic substances, in USA as well as Europe.

Another wave of recognition was ignited by Terence Mckenna who popularized his enthusiasm for DMT's incredible potential around the 80's and 90's, when he extensively explored and documented the substance, while also traveling to get to know its Amazonian origins and the traditional manners in which indigenous people used it.

It took thirty years for the story of DMT to come back to the public eye, but this time it was going to hit the front pages and become a mainstream phenomenon. It all happened in the 90's when Rick Strassman started to research further the effects that hallucinogens produce in our brains, enhancing perception, and essentially expanding our consciousness. After delivering a number of studies on the subjective response to this type of substance in different individuals, including the outputs of different doses, in the year 2000 he published 'The Spirit Molecule', a book that is still the main reference in any discussion about DMT.

The book was followed by a documentary, in 2010, that the director Mitch Schultz did in collaboration with Dr. Strassman, and which paved the way for an entire culture surrounding the DMT phenomenon. DMT was gaining adepts not only among the scientists, philosophers or those concerned with researching consciousness but building a much greater audience.

'The spirit molecule' became the famous nickname of dimethyltryptamine, and this indicated another level of public awareness in regards to this compound that was known earlier in the sixties as 'the businessman's trip' due to its short time effect and lack of after-effects when coming back. Its new label marked DMT's upgrading from a drug substance to a consciousness expanding compound.

Extensive research into DMT was produced also by the famous chemists Alexander and Anna Shulgin, who have synthesized, experimented with and documented most of the psychotropic substances that are now illegally used, as well as legally studied and employed in therapy worldwide. 'Tihkal' is the name of their publication in which they talk about the effects of tryptamines when smoked or consumed orally in different dosages.

Since it became known all over the world, DMT is gaining more and more popularity, due to the scientific interest that it presents and the studies that follow, in the quest of exploring its potential use in therapy as well as an instrument to indulge into the new discipline of consciousness. The grand-scale familiarity and usage of dimethyltryptamine is owed in part to its fairly easy process of extraction, which makes it an available activity to anyone with little chemistry know-how, although it still is a Schedule 1 substance from a legal point of view.

Chemistry, Pharmacology & Effects

DMT, or N, N-dimethyltryptamine is an endogenous indole alkaloid found widely in plants and animals, pertaining to the class of tryptamines, as its analogous compounds 5-hydroxy-DMT and 5-methoxy-DMT. Its chemical structure resembles those of serotonin and melatonin, as well as other hallucinogenic substances.

DMT is said to occur naturally as a by-product of our bodies and although there is not sufficient proof to clearly determine this, it's been discovered within our bodies in enough concentrations to suggest it does have a specific role. According to the well-known myth concerning the inherent production of DMT by our bodies, it is supposedly generated by the pineal gland. There's insufficient evidence to state this as a fact in humans, but DMT has been found in the pineal gland of rats.

DMT's synthesis within our bodies starts from tryptophan that becomes tryptamine and then with the action of INMT (indolethylamine-N-methyltransferase), N-methyltryptamine is created, which is finally catalyzed into DMT. INMT is mostly found in the thyroid, lungs and adrenal gland, as well as in the pineal gland, although other areas of the brain are scarce in this compound.

The trick is that these areas that are fertile for the production of DMT, are also containing the necessary enzymes that can break it down and suppress its absorption into the bloodstream. These MAO-A, monoamine oxidase A, act very rapidly, as such any trace of DMT disappears from the blood in less than an hour.

Studies have found that the main action of DMT is upon the serotonin receptors, more precisely on the 5-HT2A receptor. Researching further, it has been indicated that DMT also affects dopamine and sigma-1 receptors. Inquiring its bonding to sigma-1 receptor may bring significant clues in explaining the role of the naturally occurring DMT, otherwise the mystery of why our bodies produce this substance prevails over all assumptions.

The sigma-1, receptor which is detected throughout our bodies, is ensuring that our cells don't die in low oxygen situations, whereof this can be the basis of the theory that DMT is generated in abundance when we die in a desperate attempt to resurrect the dying cells. In this line of thought, the body appears to give itself an overdose of DMT in order to survive, providing us with the psychedelic experience as collateral. This would explain why a lot of subjects who have experienced near-death reported mystical encounters, a state of detachment and profound spiritual awareness.

The effects are wide ranging, starting from a generally uplifting sensation that can be described as euphoria of the mind, body and heart. In this sense, it should be stated that it accelerates the heart rate, and generally, this is the down-side in terms of negative side-effects.

On a physical level, DMT induces a sense of spatial disorientation, and with the detachment from the body comes as well a disruption in sensing temperature, and distortion of gravity, one can feel as light as a feather and be propelled light-years away in a matter of fractions of seconds.

As for the mental effects, there are a plethora of symptoms, from the ego death that we've discussed earlier to cognitive euphoria and a substantial improvement of the analytical function, to delusion and deja-vu sensations. A state of mindfulness is induced, where the memory of individuality disappears, and in this state, novelty is welcomed and appreciated as it's bringing along the total refresh of consciousness.

Mind capacity is essentially expanded such as to contain multiple streams of thought in a dynamic structure that flows freely in the absence of time and space. In a bad trip all these aspects can be reversed in anxiety and paranoia when the actual trip cannot be contained as a temporary experience and is taken with the fear of death surpassing the enthusiasm of the new.

The sense of sight is enhanced in a most amazing manner with the image flipping, melting and morphing in a symmetrical and repetitive pattern, with a color acuity that makes everything glow. The vision is somewhere in between digital and organic, where the perfect geometry of sharp angles collapses in round corners and soft edges, only to shift again in a complex structure. On the other hand, the sense of hearing is not affected at such extents, it is merely enhanced to a more ample set of vibrations but this is rather occurring at the end of the DMT trip.

The hallucinatory effect can manifest in a myriad of ways, but certain phenomenons are similar for every user. Be it internal or external, the visions are autonomous and interactive, lucid and transcendental, be it of spiritual, fantasy or science-fiction nature. What's most significant though from a therapeutic point of view, are the transpersonal effects, from the erasing of identity to an enhanced perception of self-meaning, understanding the existential purpose and the mechanics of consciousness, while experiencing a sense of unity and interconnectivity with everything there is.

There are a few stages that the DMT trip goes through, from the on-set that starts with an enhancement in vision and mental penetration, the forming of geometrical patterns and crackling or high pitched sounds. After breaking through you find yourself in a sort of waiting room or rather waiting channel, as it seems more like a tunnel with rapidly shifting geometry, through which you are pushed with the speed of light until the other side.

That is where you find the parallel realities populated with the collective archetypes enriched with your own unconscious imagery. It is there where you experience the peak of your transformational journey, meeting the entities and exploring cosmic landscapes. From this point the coming back is as if you're gradually sucked away from that dimension, further and further until you reach Earth again, in which time the realms you've traveled to along with the memory itself of this experience quickly dissipates. The previous state of presence in the parallel multiverse dies out after about ten minutes, and along with it, the visions disappear as well. The trip leaves you in a state of excitement and awe, a high that you can feel in the body for almost an hour after.

Proper DMT Consumption

As with everything in our modern speedy age, we wish for everything that we do to take as a short while as possible, in a most simple manner and to leave us fresh enough to return to work, tasks, friends or whatever routine we have. For this reason 'the businessman's trip' was perfect in so many ways. It takes just a couple of minutes to take your stash of DMT crystals out of your pocket and into the pipe, heat it, inhale the vapors and in no time you are catapulted in other dimensions.

The effect takes off in less than a second. The single thing you have to take care of is your setting, you can't do it standing the way you smoke your cigarette in a break and you wouldn't want your colleagues to watch you trippin'. But other than that, in just twenty minutes from the moment you took the first deep breath in, you'll be as fresh as before, at least.

Thus, you can skip your lunch break and use it to travel light miles away, visit infinite worlds and taste eternity. Of course this mind-blowing experience would require some time to relax and contain the enormous amount of information you've just received. But nonetheless, all this visionary trance is diluted in great proportion in the few moments it takes for you to come down from the peak of the trip to the three-dimensional reality, just like the dream evaporates from your memory when you open your eyes.

There's only fragments that stay with you, glimpses to remind you that indeed you went away and it wasn't all just your vivid imagination. There's no aftereffect of dizziness, confusion or physical impairment to stop you from getting back to whatever you've been doing before, so nobody can notice anything suspect with you, or maybe just a more clear, active, present and enthusiastic attitude, but in this case, you could just blame it on the double shot espresso you just had.

Proper Preparation

Approaching this mysterious substance in the manner described above is appropriate only for the experienced users that are familiar with the substance, with the journey and are able to grasp and contain the miraculous experience with clarity and awareness. Otherwise, the recreational consumption of DMT could be a lack of respect towards the immense potential of knowledge this molecule can offer you.

Its Amazonian counterpart is taken in a complex ritual that prepares your body, but most of all, your mind, to be able to smoothly navigate the cosmic waters and integrate the gifts of this voyage in a most helpful manner.

Ayahuasca is foremost a medicine and the attitude of the indigenous people towards consuming the plant brew is accordingly, they are searching for remedies, for purifying their spirits and material bodies as well, for enlightenment and precious insights from other spirit entities they meet during the trance.

To accomplish this, a special state of being is requested and you need to be in tune, open and respectful. As such, a particular diet is recommended to cleanse your system and allow the substance to pass gently, ease the purification work of the body to let the spiritual experience to occur with grace and no impediments. Extra rituals with different purgative plants are usually performed before the Ayahuasca ceremony, like tobacco tea that makes you release the toxins out of your body through vomiting, or using an even more powerful compound as the venom of the Cambo frog that has the same purpose and a much powerful effect.

Of course these procedures are necessary because the Amazonian concoct activates through your digestive system and the more cluttered it is, the harder for the medicine to make its way. The whole hallucinogenic trance is affected by the hops and blockages which are in return reflected in not so pleasant visions.

This is because, as we all know by now, everything within us is connected, it's just that we are not yet able to translate this properly, so an upset bowel can be seen as a furious dragon and, while caught up in distant unknown worlds, you may just miss it and confuse it for what it is not.

In the case of DMT that needs no digestion to take effect inside your body and mind, this type of preparation becomes superfluous. However, what 'the businessman' bypasses in the whole process is that the period of physical preparation constitutes a chance to prepare your consciousness for the leap of faith that DMT, as Ayahuasca, offers.

It represents a time in which you concentrate your full awareness on freeing old unbalanced mind-patterns and setting out in the journey with clear intentions. The toxins in your body make your brain foggy and confused which may induce anxiety, fear and miss-judgment, for which reasons the Amazonians use purging on a regular basis. You could say it's almost like plucking the weeds and preparing the soil to be fertile enough to nurture and grow the new seeds you're about to plant.

Knowing the stages of this process that the South Americans perfected in a very long time of constant work with the plant medicine, can give you an idea about the manner in which you should approach any substance that has the potential of a psychotropic healing experience. So, unless you're the type of businessman that devotedly practices his daily transcendental meditation and are therefore able to enter a mindful state by the clap of your hands, it would be recommended to take some time off and prepare yourself a ritualic setting of the interior and exterior space before you indulge in inhaling DMT.

Instruments & Techniques

DMT in the form of crystals can be smoked or vaporized, but either way it is highly important for the flame not to touch the compound such as not to lose its potency in the air before it gets in your lungs.

You can use a freebase pipe, or meth pipe, in which case you put the crystals directly in the bulb, then heat up the glass to vaporize the substance and inhale it. Keep the smoke in for 10-20 seconds, then breathe out and repeat the process. A more efficient instrument is the glass vapor genie that practically ensures you there's no loss of DMT in the heating or burning and that it all gets inside your system.

The most common way to consume DMT is the sandwich method, in which you place the DMT crystals in between the leaves of a plant, be it marijuana or another plant and put it in a pipe or a bong. Proceeding in this manner will necessitate much more attention as you have to be careful to merely heat the upper leaves and not burn them. It's the simplest method when you don't have other more adequate equipment but it leaves room for so many errors that you will have to be prepared with extra DMT material to refill in order to truly get a breakthrough. What you can do to increase the efficiency is to create a gravity bong so as to pile up the smoke inside and take a full inhalation at the end.

Another more sophisticated process is to enhance the plant leaves with DMT, or in simpler words, to infuse the inactive plant with a DMT solution and afterward smoke it. This is done by immersing the DMT and plant in a solvent, be it isopropyl alcohol, butane or acetone, leave it and wait patiently for a few days till the solvent evaporates, and only afterward consume it. This is very similar to the substance that goes by the name changa, but this plant mix uses an addition of a MAOI containing herb that prolongs the experience. Plants like blue Lotus, Passionflower or Caapi are used, but as the testimonials report, even though the effect goes on for a considerable longer period, the high is substantially less strong.

Important Tip

Either way you choose, there's one essential aspect that you have to remember and this is advice from experienced users, something Terence Mckenna repeated with each and every occasion. When you feel you're about to take off, take one more big inhalation. That and only that will do the job. Otherwise you'd just get a glimpse of the other unearthly worlds, a mere check out from the window and not have enough propulsion to fly off this planet.

This is a mistake most first time users make when they don't have proper guidance. If you don't do it in the right time, which is right away, then you will have to wait for a while for MAO-A to clear out of your system as otherwise the DMT you consume will be immediately broken down without any chance of transforming into the miraculous voyage you're so eagerly expecting.

Extraction

Most common plants out of which DMT is extracted are the root barks of Acacia Confusa or Mimosa Hostilis, although there is a great number of other herbs that can be used. The variety of extraction methods are able to suit any level of chemistry knowledge. The simplest is to take the grounded plant matter and immerse it into a base solution, usually sodium hydroxide, which literally dissolves the plant and leaves the DMT molecules floating in the liquid.

To separate the DMT, a non-polar solvent is added in order to attract the non-polar DMT molecules out of the polar base you've just used. The non-polar solvent, now containing the DMT molecules, separates itself in a different layer and can be easily siphoned out of the base solution. In the end, through evaporation or freezing, you can liberate the DMT molecules out of the solvent, leaving you with the crystals that are ready to be heated and inhaled.

Entering The Hallway Of All Possible Realities

Each DMT journey is unique not only from one individual to another, but also the trips of the same person greatly differ from each other. You can say it is like entering another door each time you take this substance, which can be said as well about other psychedelics, but in the case of DMT the endeavor is so incredible that it seems like completely distinct lifetimes altogether. You feel like a different entity each time around.

In all instances you experience the multiverse, the infinite parallel realities merging into each other, morphing in unimaginable forms and colors, in patterns that dissipate and rearrange constantly at high speeds, in front of your very eyes and throughout your body. You feel you are one with everything that is occurring, not only participating but existing in each and every geometric frame, dissolving with it and transforming into something else. And everything goes on indefinitely, all over the cosmos.

In these completely unknown and spectacular worlds where DMT takes you, you most curiously feel at home, for they're all entangled with our common reality, there's no sensation of rupture, it is all but one grand existence. This phenomenon fills you with a feeling of sacredness, with the impression that you are experiencing the very essence of life in a context much bigger than life itself.

It is therefore the spiritual awakening to a grander awareness in which you could literally say that you are meeting all virtual gods and most of all the god within. The sensation is that there is no difference between you and these sanctified entities, you are one of them. You are living the eternity in the infinity of space, and nothing gives off the suspicion of an illusion, instead it seems much more real than the reality we are accustomed to. You are being detached from your body, your senses, your memories, your entire self, and continuing to sense and understand through your consciousness.

In these distant realms you meet with different light entities that most often than not, welcome you with warmth and loving vibrations to their worlds, showing you around and inviting you to get a taste of the infinite. They are the most curious characters that not even your dreams have shown something similar.

They come in a variety of sizes and shapes, they sometimes have strawberry heads and machine like bodies, much like the well-known syntagm that Mckenna was using to describe his guides, the 'self-transforming machine elves'. There's always this combination between something digital and something organic, yet each time a slightly distinct god-like creature appearing in sight.

Even though it may not be of the same flesh and blood we're familiar with, it's nonetheless more real than our own bodies that we've just left behind. In this context, with you not having a body to structure your visible image in this multiverse, you may be wondering how do you look like for them. Maybe you're not wearing your usual humanoid cloak, maybe you also have an unbelievably wild and miraculous form just like them.

These friendly entities are your guides in the journey and besides giving you an unforgettable ride, they also work on your light body, giving you precious existential advice that has the potential of turning your life around. This is why most users confess they consume DMT for its therapeutic properties because they come back from their trips endorsed with powerful knowledge on what is good and meaningful for them.

Most DMT reports account for the meeting of a female or a male guide, a voice or even a character that leads them in their journeys. These guides are showing them the grand potential that lies within each, how to tap into this source of energy and use it for their own benefit, as well as for the greater good of humanity and life throughout the universes.

The interesting fact is that men usually encounter the female voice, and women the male's, which takes us to Carl Jung's theories of soul, who states that each man's soul is the Anima, the female within him, and each woman's soul is the Animus, the male within her. There's more connections between the DMT voyage and Jung's visions, for he talks extensively about the realm of the collective unconscious where all the figures that have ever populated the imagination and mythology of humankind, are gathered.

Whereof the dimensions that DMT discloses seem to be exactly that, with the only correction that the machine-like entities are nowhere to be found in the history of human thoughts and fantasies, they surpass all philosophies, religions and fairytales. In this sense, we may say that the DMT trip immerses us in collective universal consciousness of infinitely greater extents than our human unconscious.

DMT vs Other Psychedelics

Continuing the subject discussed just above concerning the realms one visits and entities one encounters during the DMT journey, we may start comparing it with its South American counterpart with which it shares most similarities, the Ayahuasca brew. The Amazonian plant medicine, in fact, draws much closer to Jung's theories in that it discloses precisely the fairytale lands of dreams and the archetypes that we got to know from fairytales, myths and other stories of that type.

For once, the Ayahuasca is known to echo the spirit of Mother Earth that comes embodied in a huge anaconda snake, a dragon-like appearance that seems to be the guide of the inner journey. The other spirits one meets during the eight hour voyage are all in one way or other familiar faces, presenting similitudes with something we've always known deep inside.

Although it is an extraordinary experience, the resemblances connect us with something from our memory, thus with our individuality and the collective individuality of humankind. For this reason, the whole journey is a very personal one, which brings forth the fears and anxieties tormenting the soul. On the contrary, with DMT, everything is so spectacularly new that you don't get the chance to sense fear, except the fear of novelty, of the unknown, of astonishment, not inner conflicts.

This also means that from a therapeutic point of view, the Amazonian plant medicine presents itself as a more efficient

healer because it works directly with your problems. The anaconda travels within your being and spits out the blockages, the unresolved tensions, the sickness, cleansing your entity in its way out.
The duration of the whole experience is important in this aspect as well, as DMT is way shorter. We must also address the action upon the body: while DMT seems to have no physical effect, Ayahuasca makes you purge out all the accumulated toxins. The Curanderos of South America are praising specifically this property of the brew, putting higher importance on the purge than the visions it reveals, for the cleansing process is actually the healing one.

Going further, we may classify between the organic psychedelics and the synthesized substances, and present the fact that compounds as magic mushrooms, Ayahuasca, Iboga, Peyote, although very different from each other, they all come with a spirit guide that has origins in the nature of our planet, a spirit that you most definitely feel vibrating within you.

On the contrary, DMT, much like LSD are very different in this aspect, calling on entities that seem out of this realm, and often coming with no other guidance than your own consciousness. The senses of perception are very different especially because of the nature of the substance, wherein the synthesized compounds bring forth a more digital visualization of reality, resembling the structure of our modern culture and current imagery.

There are no 'self-transforming machine elves' in the magic mushroom trip unless you bring them in from your past DMT journey. In the DMT trip the digital and organic elements combine in one whole image of reality, and this seems to be a more truthful vision of reality as one unified consciousness field. The more we explore these other dimensions, the more we co-create, the more borders and differences between these realities melt and merge.

The main aspects that separate DMT from all the others and make it absolutely unreal, is the great potency and incredibly short duration. One LSD trip takes about 3-4 hours, a stronger magic mushroom experience can last 6-7 hours, whereas the journey on Ayahuasca or Peyote is 8-9 hours long, and an Iboga session can keep you in trance for more than 12 hours. In this context, the DMT journey seems to compress a whole universe in just one dot, the essence.

It resembles only one other compound and that is Salvia Divinorum, which as well takes off instantly and is over after 5-10 minutes. Unlike DMT, though, this type of sage is usually said to bring horrific visions of a distorted reality and the sense of detachment from your body. The physical plane is replaced with the disfiguration of the carnal and material informs that you not only you see but also feel.

There is no other psychotropic substance to catapult you out of this planet like DMT, to infuse you with exclusively novel information and sensations, to bridge unknown realities with a warm and peaceful welcoming. Of course this makes the journey more of an exploratory one than a therapeutic enterprise because it occupies your consciousness with a state of awe instead of pointing it towards the problems within your own body and psyche, which need your attention.

It directs your awareness outwards instead of inwards as the psychedelics do. You don't get to consciously confront your troubles because you simply forget about all of them, along with everything else related to your material existence. The therapy nonetheless happens in the background and with your conscious effort only after the trip is over. That is to say that it does take more energy and concentration to understand the teachings that you've received in your journey and implement the necessary changes in your daily life and in this physical reality.

On the opposite side though, the longer trips on Ayahuasca, Peyote and even LSD put you in front of your issues and you are supposed to resolve them during the trip. Most emotional or psychological blockages have to be dealt with at the beginning of the journey such as to smoothly take off and not get stuck in a loop. For this reason, the DMT interstellar voyages are generally much more peaceful and there's less potential of having a bad trip. If you're being honest to yourself, you'd have to admit that all bad trips are nothing else than violent confrontations with fears or unresolved intimate issues, and the DMT trance simply happens to fast.

DMT Culture

The great body of literature that grew around this mind-blowing mysterious compound has been greatly connected with the grand culture of psychedelics that was born in the sixties. The psychedelic revolution generated an enhancement of perception in a period of liberation from social inhibiting judgments and predetermined forms of thought. It coincided with a fruitful period for human beings when spiritual practices from the East were imported to evolve the pragmatic man of the West. Psychedelic substances played a great role in the rebirth of humanity and the expanding of our collective consciousness such as to receive bright new existential insights.

As such, a lot of the great minds of the period, philosophers, artists and scientists alike engaged in the experimenting with psychotropic substances in clinic environments but also illegally in their own homes, setting the stage for what was to become the study of consciousness.

The books that have been written in that period treat the psychedelic experience in its whole, as it was the new kid on the block, so new that it was hard to discern among its multitude of expressions. Chemists, Shulgin and Hoffman, the discoverers of LSD, were mostly concentrated on studying the visible spectrum of effects and noting each of them along with the respective dosages and chemical interactions.

When it came to the subtle differences in perception and awareness that each psychedelic substance induced, most of the researchers used to talk about the great effect of all of them, too slightly differentiating between their particularities, for it was one grand phenomenon bursting in the human reality all of a sudden, producing such a major shift that none could be something more than the other. As such, most writings about DMT are to be found among the greater presentation of psychedelics in general.

The great prophet of the psychedelic revolution was Timothy Leary, Harvard psychologist and author of the book titled 'High Priest', a precious introduction into the culture of the times, written while he was in and out of jail on reasons concerning exactly the use and promotion of psychedelics. He particularly discusses his own DMT trip as well as other accounts in an article titled 'Programmed communication during experiences with DMT', published in the 'Psychedelic Review'. It is all about breaking the set patterns of perception in order to free your consciousness, as Aldous Huxley praises in his famous novel 'The doors of perception', and as other famous figures as Alan Watts preach in their teachings.

Terence Mckenna, whom we've mentioned quite a few times in this book, was utterly fascinated with DMT. Not as much as he was with psychedelic mushrooms, but still enough to talk for hours on end and write tons of pages about. He was thinking about the 'paradox that DMT is the most powerful yet most harmless of all substances' and being impressed with how 'the human mind can endure that much beauty'.

One of the great figures of our contemporary period discussing DMT is Graham Hancock, who's written and lectured extensively about this compound. His view is that DMT grants us the unique possibility of getting in contact with sentient beings out of our reality, beings that we are otherwise completely unaware of. These entities however know about us and have precious insights that would not only expand our consciousness but also enrich our material lives and provide extraordinary understandings on how to co-create our common reality within the multiverse.

Therapeutic Effects On Anxiety & Depression

As we've talked about, the DMT trip does not directly confront you with the source of your imbalance, rather it takes a more divergent route, presenting you with bewildering settings and characters that don't give you the chance to concentrate on anything else besides that.

In this aspect, it is so much different than Ayahuasca, mushrooms or LSD, substances that are employed in therapy nowadays and that have an obvious action within the psyche apart from the chemical effect within the body. These latter psychedelics induce a psychological trance that is very similar to a therapy session with a psychologist, where you travel inside your own mind, confront and discuss the issues that appear problematic. With DMT, we cannot talk about such action, but nevertheless, this compound has its own means of re-stating the balance within your being.

Recent medical studies inquired a specific strand of DMT, 5-MeO-DMT, commonly found in a lot of plants, but mostly extracted from the venom of the Bufo Alvarius frog. The experiments with this compound on a great number of subjects proved that with only one or two administrations, there was a huge improvement in their overall well-being, with the levels of anxiety and depression decreasing in ways that no other medication or therapy provided before.

The essential advancement that DMT brings forth in comparison with the therapy that engages other psychedelic substances is the duration of the whole trip. While the magic mushrooms effect, which is now the first in line of research in this matter, takes about nine hours, DMT succeeds in doing at least as good of a job in only half an hour to at most an hour and a half, and this is of major importance for someone who is suffering from acute conditions.

Studies have been undergone regarding the new trend of microdosing, and DMT was administered in microdoses on rats to explore how they react. Indeed, after a little more than a month the rats showed signs of decreased levels of anxiety when inquiring their reactions to fear and past traumas. But there were as well side effects, in that the male rats inexplicably gained weight, whereof the female rats suffered important changes in their neural structures and lost spine density. These studies are only the very first steps in the investigation of DMT though, as this compound is one of the most recent psychedelics to be researched for new medicine.

Nevertheless, if we take just a glimpse on the countless reports of DMT users it might give us a more general and authentic perspective than the precise medical studies. Most of the users confess to an unprecedented improvement on their states of being after consuming DMT, and many of them are approaching this substance specifically in an attempt to heal their anxiety and depression. For all of these, the DMT sessions with full dosage, not microdosing over a longer period, proved to be extremely effective, with this compound being a catalyst for the necessary positive changes that each have to make in their own lives.

DMT helps you find your place in the multiverse, in the multiple parallel realities that coexist with ours, and expand your mind in such a manner that you get to figure out just what's wrong with your current standpoint and the measures you need to take to rebalance in accordance with the overall reality.

From the background, it reassembles the pieces for you to take on a path of love, peace and lightness, instead of being submerged in heavy past traumas. In this sense, the phenomenon of the ego death is extremely important for it reveals that you are much more than the mental structure impeding your happiness, and helping you go beyond it, in a state where you are able to truly manifest your whole self.

Bad Trips

It is common knowledge that bad trips on psychedelics, despite their horrific appearance, are actually the most beneficial experiences and present a higher healing potential than the desirable good trips. This is because they are digging out your problems and actually providing solution and relief.

Moreover, you are the one that does all the work so the efficiency of this self-therapy is almost guaranteed, not to mention, the blissful feeling that you most necessarily receive after surviving such an experience, which makes you treasure life in all its complex manifestation.

On DMT, bad trips are a bit different, because it is all concentrated in a very short amount of time and the sensation of being detached from this material reality bypasses the chance of actually connecting the bad trip to some specific problem that you have.

Yes, you may meet unfriendly entities in disrupting environments during your travels, but most of the time the shock is just too big to truly scare you, it's more like watching a very vivid horror movie. More often than not, the bad trip occurs when you haven't paid enough attention to setting this psychotropic experience in a ritualic scenario, that is when you don't show respect towards this worthy substance. Set and setting are essential for all psychedelic endeavors and are the first aspects one has to take care of in the preparation for this journey.

As such, it is preferable to take DMT in a space where you feel most comfortable and calm, in a tidy atmosphere that can ensure your peace of mind, where you don't get interrupted in the middle of the trip. The synergy that DMT induces connects you profoundly with everything around you, so your own home where all is familiar and warm could be a perfect setting.

Nature can also offer a most tranquil environment in which you can immerse safely. On the contrary, if you're not looking for powerful sensations, it wouldn't be advisable to choose an abandoned setting or the club scene. As a matter of fact, most bad trips appear when people use DMT recreationally, ignorant of its huge potential, searching for some glitter when hanging out with their friends and meeting monsters instead.

Spiritual hygiene is the concept that is encompassing all the necessary preparations that you need to do in order to avoid unnecessary unpleasant situations. To summarize its meaning, it is about balancing your state of mind through meditation and setting clear intentions for the voyage you are about to undertake.

The syntagm 'desperate situations require desperate measures' does not go well with the DMT experience, so when you find yourself in an anxiety attack, DMT is not the relief pill for sure. Of course there are a lot of reports from people that were in highly depressive states and took DMT for comfort, receiving enlightening insights which uplifted their grief, but these are exceptions. The point is that whatever the context, you need to be conscious of your actions and assume as your responsibility all that comes towards you.

One other instance when bad trips can occur while doing DMT, like with other psychedelics, is when you don't leave enough time between two different journeys, two different doses. After you've had a psychedelic experience it's advisable to wait a while until you try it again; it's a sign of disrespect towards yourself and towards the trip itself if you rush things, for you didn't offer enough time for the experience to settle, for the understanding to ground inside your being.

Sometimes however, you have bad trips despite your preparation efforts, so you can learn to enjoy them as well. The most important lesson is not to resist the bad trip but accept it, for if you resist it, it will only come at you more forcefully. It may also help to open your eyes and remind yourself that it is just a trip, that you've consumed a psychedelic substance and in a while it will all pass, and you will return to your normal state of being.

Another beneficial piece of advice comes from Terence Mckenna, who, in his turn, borrowed it from the South American shamans, and that is to sing. Whenever a beast like creature that frightens you appears in your scenario, sing to it. When you feel distorted out of recognition, just sing. Whatever comes to mind, sing.

And most of all, do not combine DMT with alcohol or other drugs. This is a recipe for disaster as you will have less control over your thoughts and actions that could lead to poor or dangerous scenarios.

The Cure For Collective Awareness?

We look at our lives irresponsibly in regards to our true nature and we treat the planet in a similar manner as if we are not all connected in the same collective reality. Who are we kidding? We constantly hide our true problems under the carpet, behind the screens of our devices, ignorant to the fact that they don't just disappear and to the harm they are doing to us in the background.

We tend to only choose comfort, and avoid bad trips when it is discomfort and nasty experiences that truly define our reality. What if we chose to confront all these? Maybe it wouldn't be a better world overnight, but it may sure be a more honest attitude.

Of course it takes courage to do this, especially when you feel you are facing the whole of reality by yourself. DMT can show you that you are much larger than you could ever imagine, that you are much more than the social stance that's been imprinted on you, that your role in the whole equation of reality is way more important than the job you are doing or the status you've achieved in your community, that the actual reality is much greater than the most brilliant minds who have defined it. You are important for the simple fact that you exist and that all is interconnected.

DMT might prove to be the most necessary source of wisdom in our fragmented times, the link that can finally dissolve duality and with it the paradox of existence that is making us constantly take sides. This is because it reveals that there are infinite angles and not just two, as humanity has been accustomed to seeing all in black and white.

DMT is finally dissolving this duality, mainly by resolving the conflict between spirituality and science. As we've seen earlier, the beliefs in a greater dimension of reality, as well as in life after death and the facts demonstrated by quantum physics are both reflected in the DMT experience. By transcending duality we may get the ticket to enter another stage in the human evolution, that of a unified reality, and with it, unified humanity.

DMT has the power of awakening the consciousness of the soul inside the individual to the reality that truly is a multiverse of interconnected beings. By this, it awakens the responsibility that each of us has towards their own wellbeing, and towards the wellbeing of our collective environment, which translates in the health of our planet as well as the peace of our collective mental and emotional dimensions. Through such a short glimpse into the complexity of our dynamics, DMT succeeds to truly wake up our spirit and our consciousness.

Thank you for reading! I hope you enjoyed the book and if you learnt anything or thought it was an interesting journey it would mean the world if you could leave a review! Thank you in advance :)

Also if you enjoyed this you might enjoy my other book 'An Introductory Guide To Magic Mushrooms - The Beginners Psychedelic Explorer's Guide Of This Hallucinogenic Plant'. Below is a sample of some of the popular pages of the book.

Bonus: An Introductory Guide To Magic Mushrooms
The Beginners Psychedelic Explorer's Guide Of This Hallucinogenic Plant

Frequently asked questions

These are all your frequently asked questions, at a glance.
Well, some of you might want a quick overview of mushrooms and tripping. While we in no way promote the use of illegal drugs, we all have a responsibility to know the facts.

Are mushrooms addictive?
No, mushrooms are generally not recorded as being addictive. Tolerance for mushrooms builds up after repeated usage so, generally speaking, mushrooms do not encourage repeated use in a short space of time. There is always the chance that you become addicted to the experience of tripping, taking mushrooms, or experimenting with them.

Some people develop a lifelong fascination with them, growing them or becoming experts on various strains, types and experiences. There are people who have made a career from this or have become expert bloggers, writers or scientists on the topic.

Are there drugs tests for magic mushrooms?
Psilocybin, the active properties in magic mushrooms, turns into psilocin. This can be found in urine and hair samples. Traces of magic mushrooms disappear pretty quickly. In urine, it is normally gone within a few hours, maximum 24 or, in cases of chronic doses or overuse, 48 hours. It can remain

in your blood for 1-2 days but normally disappears pretty quickly compared to other substances.

How do magic mushrooms affect the brain?
Magic mushrooms affect the brain through the chemical compounds attaching themselves to serotonin (happy) receptors in the brain. They alter consciousness by disrupting thought patterns and changing the normal signal patterns around your brain, meaning that you perceive reality in a different way, often processing visual and sensory information in new ways.

Can magic mushrooms be spiked or laced?
Because of their appearance (mushroom-shaped!), they are unlikely to be cut with other drugs. However, some reports have suggested that normal mushrooms have been sold to unsuspecting people and that some of these are laced with LSD instead of organically containing the psychoactive properties of mushrooms, psilocybin. Also, if they are crushed and dried/in pill form, you will not know what is inside or whether they are cut with something else.

How long does a trip last?
A trip generally lasts between 4-6 hours when the mushrooms are eaten. It takes between 30-60 minutes to come up.

What do magic mushrooms look like?
With over 180 psilocybin containing mushroom species out there, it is impossible to summarise what magic mushrooms look like specifically. However, what they have in common is that they have a cap and a stem and gills underneath. Their color varies considerably. Many of them are very easily

confused with poisonous varieties and spore prints have to be taken in order to identify them correctly.

How do magic mushrooms make you feel?
Magic mushrooms have an effect on the central nervous system. How they make you feel is very much dependent on you. They can induce euphoria-like feelings, visual sensations, an altered sense of time and space but also, in some cases, anxiety or nervousness.

Are magic mushrooms dangerous?
As things go, magic mushrooms are generally considered 'safe' in chemical terms. Their danger lies in triggering psychotic episodes if you have mental health disorders. In very rare cases they can cause prolonged anxiety. They generally do not result in death unless dangerous activity is carried out whilst under the influence. They are not as known to cause flashbacks (as in the case of LSD).

How are mushrooms stored?
Once picked, mushrooms remain fresh from between five and ten days, depending entirely on their water content. You can store them in the fridge. However, like any living organism, they can rot if left longer. If not, you can put them into a container or sealed bag and freeze them for around 7 months to one year. Many people choose to dry them for use much later on. This is most people's preferred option. Psilocybin mushroom potency is reduced through drying but not by a significant amount at all.

How do you dry mushrooms?
Drying them can be achieved by letting them air dry on a piece of paper or speeding up the process by drying them on

a piece of paper on a radiator. After you have dried them, it is best to put them in an airtight container, although you should be aware that their strength will gradually decrease over time. You can also put them in an oven with the door open or in an oven with the door closed (as long as the temperature does not go over 95 Fahrenheit/ 36 degrees).

How do you prepare magic mushrooms?
This is entirely up to the person taking them but most people prefer tea as it is gentler on the stomach. Be careful not to boil the water but to just stew the mushrooms in warm water. You can add herbs, flavorings or herbal tea to improve on the taste. When mushrooms are picked fresh, they should be rinsed before consumption.

Can you eat mushrooms as they are?
Mushrooms are also eaten fresh or dried, however, this can cause stomach cramps and vomiting, and the taste is unpleasant, so most people prefer to brew tea.

How many magic mushrooms do you need to trip?
This is varied depending on the type/strain.
Liberty Caps dried require 1-3 for medium, and 3-7 for strong, or 2-18 fresh for a moderate trip and 7 to 42 fresh for a strong one. *Cubensis* require 1-3 dried, or 2-7 for a stronger trip. For *cubensis* that are fresh, the maximum dose for a very strong trip is up to 28g fresh. These are very rough guidelines.

What is it like to trip?
Tripping can be euphoric, visual and cause altered consciousness. Throughout the duration, you may oscillate between happy feelings, panicky, relaxed, insular, thoughtful and creative.

Should you take other drugs with mushrooms?
It is inadvisable to take other drugs with magic mushrooms. Some people take cannabis alongside it which they say can reduce sickness at the start for the first hour. However, cannabis can also increase anxiety and panic which could combine with the mushrooms. There are reports online of people going overboard and being pulled in many different directions by a cocktail of substances. Amphetamines (speed) and cocaine are especially to be avoided. They just don't go. We discuss this in more detail on the mixology section in this guide.

What do mushrooms do to the brain?
After the psilocybin is converted to psilocin in the body, it is pumped to the brain where it increases a type of serotonin (5HT-2A) – which controls the neural transmission of things affecting mood, perception, memory, awareness and appetite.

What are the after effects? (Comedowns)
After effects of mushrooms, comedowns, are not really a major feature of the drug. As we saw with trip report 3, some people experience psychological effects triggered by the mushrooms themselves, but there is nothing necessarily chemical that occurs. The day after taking mushrooms, people can generally feel tired or a little confused, or things and experiences that have occurred during the tripping itself can stay with you (good or bad). Comedowns as to the sort felt on ecstasy or MDMA are not as comparable.

www.ingramcontent.com/pod-product-compliance
Lightning Source LLC
Chambersburg PA
CBHW071323080526
44587CB00018B/3330